Fern Green

photographs by Deirdre Rooney

CONTENTS

INTRODUCTION

Tea is a hot drink made from dried or fresh leaves that has been drunk for thousands of years. Western cultures tend to separate tea into drinks made with the tea plant and those with herbal infusions.

The tea plant, *Camellia sinensis*, is the main ingredient in the world's most popular beverage. Herbal tea or infusions are made from fresh or dried leaves, herbs, flowers, berries, seeds, roots, rhizomes or bark infused in hot water. They are caffeine free.

Green Tea and Tonics is a beginner's book for people who want to get the health benefits of herbs into their diet with no additives, preservatives or dyes. And, of course, for those who would like to extend their tea-making repertoire. The recipes are made from tea leaves, herbs, spices and fruits enabling you to try new flavours and variations of a popular drink.

The importance of water

Water plays a vital role in increasing the effectiveness of tea. Water is essential to the body for the absorption of nutrients. It diffuses the potency of the herb and delivers its properties in a manner that is complementary to the body's natural processes.

How to make the best tea

When making tea, try following these steps to help you achieve a perfect cup of tea.

- Use fresh, organically grown leaves or flowers. Dried herbs (dried in the shade) can also be used, as long as they are no more than 10 months old.

- Carefully wash any herbs, flowers or leaves that you use from the garden.

- Use a clean teapot.

- Bruise any roots or seeds to release essential oils.

- Pour over boiling water and cover with a lid immediately. You can use the same ingredients for one or two more brews.

- Steep for up to 5 minutes, then pour through a strainer into a cup or mug and sip.

Tea steeping times

These can vary depending on what tea or herbal blend you are making, but here is a rough guide.

White – *The purest and least processed of the teas. Air-dried and slightly oxidised. Steep time: 1–3 minutes.*

Oolong – *Partly oxidised with a deep, sweet and fragrant flavour. Similar to black tea. Steep time: 3–5 minutes.*

Green – *Toasted, steamed or dried to prevent oxidation and to lock in colour and the grassy flavour. Steep time: 3–5 minutes.*

Black – *It's the darkest and the strongest tea. Steep time: 3–5 minutes.*

Pu-erh – *Aged and fermented and sold by the vintage. Steep time: 3–5 minutes.*

Herbal – *Fresh or dried herbs, spices and flowers. Steep time: 3–5 minutes. If using bark and seeds, allow to steep for 5 minutes.*

Never use any plant as a tea unless you are 100% sure of its identification.

Tea becomes more flavourful as the tea expands, which can be hard if the leaves are tightly packed in a small bag. Using an infuser or a large mug or jam jar to steep your leaves will ensure they float around and give a better flavour.

Equipment

There is a wide selection of tea gadgets out there but as tea is meant to be a simple process, here is a list of basic equipment, which you might find helpful.

Kettle or saucepan
If you only need hot water, boil your kettle. This is the quickest and easiest way to get boiling water. If, however, you need to boil the herbs or spices, use a saucepan on the stove.

Nylon sieve
Great for straining your tea through – the nylon sieve picks up every flake and helps produce a fine clear tea.

Spoon infuser
A spoon-sized metal infuser opens to fit dried herbs inside and closes to put in a tea cup. It has holes on the sides of the spoon to release the properties into the water, without the bulk.

Strainer infuser
A circular plastic spoon infuser has strainers on both sides to allow the tea to be made with less bulk in the water.

Tea balls
These are available in most health food stores and markets. It's a small egg-shaped infuser with holes in the sides and a chain to float herbs in a cup or teapot.

Teapot
Very necessary, as all good teas need somewhere to steep. It can be replaced by a Kilner jar (or other airtight container) if you need to steep in the refrigerator overnight.

HOW TO MAKE YOUR TEAS & TONICS

Fresh herbal teas can be fun. If you are making a tea with fresh petals, stems or leaves, cut into small pieces and use 2 tablespoons of herbs per cup. Pour freshly boiled water over the herbs and steep. However, if you are making a blend with dried herbs, use 1 teaspoon of the dried herbs mix in equal parts. If you are making a blend with teabags, which usually contain around 1 teaspoon in each bag, add 1 cup of boiling water per bag. You can also combine a teabag and dried herbs in the same blend, just add more water to account for the increased potency.

Points to remember

If you are making teas from fresh garden herbs, there are a few precautions to bear in mind:

- Never pick herbs in the wild as you do not know whether the area was sprayed with chemical insecticides.

- Make sure a neighbouring plant isn't woven into the herb you are picking.

- Be sure to use the correct parts, make sure you pick fresh and wash the herbs thoroughly.

Using herbs every day

As a general rule, use one kind of herb daily for 10 days, then give it a break of 3–4 days, then continue, repeating this pattern. Herbs are far more powerful than we realise and can accumulate within the body. So it is best to vary your herbs and take them in moderation.

Above all, enjoy this remarkable way of absorbing the health-giving properties of nature's plants. Herbs make all the difference to our health and state of mind; they lift our spirits. Relish every sip!

What is a tonic?

A tonic is a type of tea that contains more concentrated nutrients to help strengthen and energise the body. Before the popularity of pharmaceuticals, doctors prescribed tonics, which were made of all sorts of herb and spice concoctions with particular ailments in mind. In this book, a tonic is made similarly to tea but with a more concentrated amount of herbs and spices. Tonics are best sipped throughout the day in smaller quantities.

What is a cleanser?

A cleanser is a drink made up of herbs and fruits, which help cleanse the body. Cleansers can help strengthen the immune system, purify and protect the blood. They are usually made by steeping herbs and fruits in cold water, and chilling overnight.

BENEFITS OF FLOWERS & HERBS

The ingredients on this list boast many benefits for your health and are great for making teas, tonics and cleansers:

Black tea — *Comes from the same plant as green tea, but the tea leaves are exposed to oxygen turning the leaves black. Benefits include lowering the risk of heart disease, encouraging a healthy immune system and regulating blood sugar levels.*

Cinnamon — *Helps lower cholesterol and increases antioxidants. Also alleviates arthritis symptoms.*

Ginger — *Anti-histamine and anti-inflammatory properties. Eases motion sickness and is a great flavour booster.*

Green tea — *A less processed tea, therefore has a higher amount of antioxidants, specifically catechins, which help fight cell damage. As well as reducing bad cholesterol, it boosts metabolism and can have a calming effect.*

Honeysuckle — *Used in Chinese medicine, it is known to release toxins out of the body. As a great antibacterial flower, it is used to treat coughs.*

Olive leaf — *Full of antioxidants and vitamin C. It is a natural antibacterial agent which supports the body's natural defences and contributes to overall health.*

Oolong tea — *Partially oxidised leaves provide the benefits of both black and green teas with a fruity flavour. It is known to help weight management and is high in caffeine.*

Raspberry leaf — *Great herb for energy and rich in vitamins and minerals.*

Red clover — *Blood cleanser and detoxifier, it cleanses heavy metals and chemical toxicity, including those caused by the use of drugs.*

Rooibos — *Naturally caffeine free, it contains two bioflavonoids called rutin and quercetin, which block the release of histamine, a chemical our bodies produce in response to allergens. It may also have benefits for skin irritations.*

Rosemary — *Aids digestion of fats, which enhances circulation and is good for the heart.*

Sage — *Increases digestive enzymes and stimulates the liver. It also helps to lower blood sugar levels.*

Peppermint — *Helps to ease pain, headaches and tension.*

Vanilla & anise — *Both of these herbs are good for curbing sweet cravings. They help to lift mood, are full of antioxidants and have a calming and soothing influence on the stomach.*

White tea — *This is the least processed tea and also has the least amount of caffeine. It can help to lower cholesterol and blood pressure and also contains antibacterial properties.*

dried raspberry leaf

black tea

red clover

ginger

rooibos tea

cinnamon

honeysuckle

rosemary

green tea

sage

peppermint

anise

olive leaf

vanilla

oolong tea

white tea

GREEN TEAS & DRIED TEAS

Here is a selection of teas that will help boost your immunity, stamina and wellbeing. There is a tea to suit every taste, from green to black, oolong, white and rooibos, with added fresh herbs and spices.

Green tea, mint & lemon verbena
Black tea, coriander & orange peel
Oolong & lemon • White tea with vanilla
Rooibos, ginger & lemon balm • Peppermint &
flaxseed • Ginger & lemon • Caraway & fennel
Cardamom, spearmint & orange peel
Cinnamon & cumin • Chamomile & allspice
Ginger, pu-erh & lime • Red clover & peppermint
Dandelion & lime peel • Comfrey & cardamom
Barley, dried cranberry & orange
Buckwheat & anise • Linden & lavender
Linden & lemon • Green tea & jasmine
Nettle tea with orange • Olive leaf tea with saffron
Iced peach rooibos tea • Raspberry leaf iced tea
Iced green tea with strawberries • Iced black tea
with orange • Iced white tea with peaches
Red clover iced tea with yuzu

GREEN TEA, MINT & LEMON VERBENA

Serves: 1 - Steeping time: 3 minutes

YOU NEED

1 teaspoon green tea or 1 teabag • 1 handful of dried mint
1 handful of dried lemon verbena • 1 teaspoon lemon juice
1 teaspoon honey, to sweeten (optional)

Green tea helps ease chronic coughs, colds and sore throats and aids the repair of cell damage.

I *Immunising*　**Di** *Diuretic*　**He** *Healing*

Pour a cup of boiling water over the herbs and lemon juice. Leave to steep for 3 minutes. Strain into a cup, add honey, if liked. Stir and sip slowly.

BLACK TEA, CORIANDER & ORANGE PEEL

Serves: 1 - Steeping time: 4 minutes

YOU NEED
1 teaspoon black tea or 1 teabag • ½ teaspoon coriander seeds, lightly crushed
5cm pared slice of orange peel • 1 teaspoon honey, to sweeten (optional)

Black tea can help reduce plaque formation.

 *Immunising* Be *Bone enhancing* Me *Mood enhancing*

Pour a cup of boiling water over the black tea, coriander seeds and orange peel. Leave for 4 minutes. Strain into a cup, add honey, if liked. Stir and sip slowly.

OOLONG & LEMON

Serves: 1 - Steeping time: 3 minutes

YOU NEED

1 teaspoon oolong tea or 1 teabag • 5cm pared slice of lemon peel

1 teaspoon lemon juice • 1 teaspoon honey, to sweeten (optional)

Oolong tea can help protect teeth against decay and helps reduce obesity and stress. Lemon can be used as a diuretic and has a high vitamin content.

Bp *Blood purifying*   **A** *Anti-inflammatory*   **Be** *Bone enhancing*

Pour a cup of boiling water over the oolong tea and lemon peel. Leave for 3 minutes. Strain into a cup, add honey, if liked, and lemon juice. Stir and sip slowly.

WHITE TEA WITH VANILLA

Serves: 1 ~ Steeping time: 5 minutes

YOU NEED
1 teaspoon white tea or 1 teabag • 1 teaspoon vanilla extract
¼ teaspoon ground cinnamon • ¼ teaspoon dried jasmine

White tea has antioxidant and anti-ageing properties that help in maintaining good health and healthy skin. Jasmine is great for relieving anxiety and tension.

D *Aids digestion* **Rx** *Relaxing* **L** *Liver cleansing*

Pour a cup of boiling water over all the ingredients and leave to steep for 5 minutes. Strain into a cup, stir and sip slowly.

ROOIBOS, GINGER & LEMON BALM

Serves: 1 - Steeping time: 4 minutes

YOU NEED

1 teaspoon rooibos tea or 1 teabag • 3 thin slices of fresh ginger
1 teaspoon dried lemon balm • 1 slice of lemon • 1 teaspoon lemon juice
3 cloves • 1 teaspoon honey, to sweeten (optional)

Rooibos is good at relieving tension and nausea, and can ease allergies.

Rx *Relaxing* **R** *Rejuvenating* **De** *Detoxifying*

Pour a cup of boiling water over tea, ginger, cloves and lemon balm. Leave for
4 minutes. Strain into a cup, add lemon slice, lemon juice and honey, if liked.
Stir and sip slowly.

PEPPERMINT & FLAXSEED

Serves: 1 - Steeping time: 5–8 minutes

YOU NEED

120g flaxseeds, crushed • 5cm peppermint sprig
2 slices of lemon • juice of ½ lemon • 5cm pared strip of lemon peel
2 teaspoons honey

This tea is great for bladder infections – drink 2 cups a day for 7 days.

D *Aids digestion* **L** *Liver cleansing* **So** *Soothing*

Pour a cup of boiling water over the flaxseeds, lemon peel and peppermint and leave to steep for 5–8 minutes. Strain into a cup, add the honey and stir. Add the juice and lemon slices, stir and sip slowly.

GINGER & LEMON

Serves: 1 - Steeping time: 5 minutes

YOU NEED

60g ginger, peeled and thinly sliced • 5cm pared strip of lemon peel

½ tablespoon lemon juice • 2 teaspoons honey

¼ teaspoon cayenne pepper (optional – particularly good for colds)

This tea is particularly good to ease a cold. Cayenne pepper is a fabulous antiseptic for the throat. Sip slowly and drink 3 cups a day for 2 days.

AC *Aids circulation*   **So** *Soothing*   **A** *Anti-inflammatory*

Pour a cup of boiling water over the ginger and crush it with the back of a teaspoon. Add remaining ingredients and stir. Leave for 5 minutes. Strain into a cup and sip.

CARAWAY & FENNEL

Serves: 1 - Simmering time: 5 minutes

YOU NEED

2 teaspoons caraway seeds • 1 teaspoon fennel seeds
5cm pared strip of lemon peel • 2 teaspoons honey
pinch of allspice • 1 teaspoon dried lemon balm

This tea helps to relieve stress and tension. Caraway seeds are a good digestive. Fennel is a good detoxifier and cleansing herb.

AR *Anxiety reducing* **D** *Aids digestion* **K** *Kidney cleansing*

Put all the ingredients, except the lemon balm, into a pan and add a cup of water. Bring to the boil then simmer for 5 minutes. Strain into a cup and add the lemon balm. Sip slowly.

CARDAMOM, SPEARMINT & ORANGE PEEL

Serves: 1 - Steeping time: 5 minutes

YOU NEED

1 teaspoon green tea or 1 teabag • 3 green cardamom pods, crushed
5cm pared strip of orange peel • 2 teaspoons dried chamomile flowers
1 fresh mint sprig

Cardamom seeds are a great digestive and are good to have after a meal.
Chamomile is known to have soothing properties.

D *Aids digestion* **C** *Calming* **A** *Anti-inflammatory*

Pour a cup of boiling water over all the ingredients and leave to steep for 5 minutes.
Strain into a cup, stir and sip slowly.

CINNAMON & CUMIN

Serves: 1 - Steeping time: 5 minutes

YOU NEED
1 cinnamon stick • 1 teaspoon caraway seeds • ½ teaspoon cumin seeds

This tea is great as a nightcap to ease menopausal symptoms.

D *Aids digestion* **Ab** *Antibacterial* **Rx** *Relaxing*

Pour a cup of boiling water over all the ingredients and leave to steep for 5 minutes. Strain into a cup, stir and sip slowly.

CHAMOMILE & ALLSPICE

Serves: 1 - Steeping time: 5 minutes

YOU NEED
1 teaspoon dried chamomile flowers • 1 teaspoon dried lemon balm
3 allspice berries, lightly cracked • ½ teaspoon honey

You can gargle with cooled chamomile tea to treat bleeding gums and mouth ulcers.

Rx *Relaxing* **So** *Soothing* **A** *Anti-inflammatory*

Pour a cup of boiling water over all the ingredients, except the honey, and leave to steep for 5 minutes. Strain into a cup, add honey and stir well. Sip slowly.

GINGER, PU-ERH & LIME

Serves: 1 - Steeping time: 5 minutes

YOU NEED
1 teaspoon pu-erh tea or 1 teabag • 60g ginger, peeled and thinly sliced
5cm pared slice of lime peel • juice of ½ lime

Pu-erh tea has antioxidant benefits and can help to lower cholesterol, blood pressure and balance blood sugar levels.

Ac *Aids circulation* **A** *Anti-inflammatory* **So** *Soothing*

Pour a cup of boiling water over all the ingredients, except the lime juice, and leave to steep for 5 minutes. Strain into a cup, add the lime juice, stir and sip slowly.

RED CLOVER & PEPPERMINT

Serves: 1 - Steeping time: 5 minutes

YOU NEED

1 teaspoon dried red clover flowers • 4 fresh peppermint sprigs

Clover can be used for the treatment of constipation. Peppermint is good for keeping the mind alert and clear.

A *Anti-inflammatory*   **D** *Aids digestion*   **L** *Liver cleansing*

Pour a cup of boiling water over all the ingredients and leave to steep for 5 minutes. Strain into a cup, stir and sip slowly.

DANDELION & LIME PEEL

Serves: 1 - Steeping time: 5 minutes

YOU NEED

1 teaspoon dried dandelion leaf • 5cm pared slice of lime peel

1 teaspoon honey

Dandelion leaves work gently and naturally to balance your bodily fluids helping prevent constipation and bloating.

Di *Diuretic*   **Cl** *Cleansing*   **D** *Aids digestion*

Pour a cup of boiling water over all the ingredients, except the honey, and leave to steep for 5 minutes. Strain into a cup and add the honey. Stir and sip slowly.

COMFREY & CARDAMOM

Serves: 1 - Steeping time: 5 minutes

YOU NEED

1 teaspoon dried comfrey leaves • 1 teaspoon dried rose petals
3 green cardamom pods, crushed • 1 teaspoon apple cider vinegar

Rose petals help with relaxation and comfrey is one of the most incredible healing plants. Do not consume this tea for longer than 10 days.

Be *Bone enhancing* **S** *Skin repairing* **Di** *Diuretic*

Pour a cup of boiling water over the comfrey leaves, petals and cardamom pods and leave for 5 minutes. Strain into a cup, add the vinegar and sip slowly while warm.

BARLEY, DRIED CRANBERRY & ORANGE

Serves: 2 - Simmering time: 2 minutes + 6 minutes boiling

YOU NEED
60g roasted barley • 1 tablespoon dried cranberries, chopped
5cm pared slice of orange peel

Barley is good in hot weather as it is known to cool the body.

A *Anti-inflammatory* **De** *Detoxifying* **K** *Kidney cleansing*

Boil the barley in a pan with 450ml water for 6 minutes. Strain through a muslin cloth. Add this back to the pan with the cranberries and orange peel and bring to the boil, then simmer for 2 minutes. Makes 2 cups of tea. Strain and sip.

BUCKWHEAT & ANISE

Serves: 1 - Steeping time: 8 minutes

YOU NEED

1 teaspoon roasted buckwheat

1 teaspoon anise, slightly crushed

Buckwheat can help stabilise blood sugar levels.

D *Aids digestion* **So** *Soothing* **Di** *Diuretic*

Pour a cup of boiling water over the buckwheat and anise and leave to steep
for 8 minutes. Strain into a cup, stir and sip slowly.

LINDEN & LAVENDER

Serves: 1 - Steeping time: 5 minutes

YOU NEED

1 teaspoon dried linden flowers • 2 thin slices of ginger
1 teaspoon dried lavender • 1 green cardamom pod • 1 teaspoon honey

This calming tea helps relax, soothe, de-stress and ease muscle tension.

Rx *Relaxing*   **Ab** *Antibacterial*   **D** *Aids digestion*

Pour a cup of boiling water over the linden, lavender, ginger and cardamom and leave for 5 minutes. Strain into a cup, add the honey and stir. Sip slowly.

LINDEN & LEMON

Serves: 1 - Steeping time: 5 minutes

YOU NEED

1 teaspoon dried linden flowers • ½ lemon, squeezed
1 teaspoon honey • 5cm pared slice of lemon peel

Linden helps alleviate indigestion.

So Soothing Di Diuretic CL Cleansing

Pour a cup of boiling water over the linden, lemon juice and lemon peel and leave to steep for 5 minutes. Strain into a cup, add the honey, stir and sip slowly.

GREEN TEA & JASMINE

Serves: 1 - Steeping time: 3–5 minutes

YOU NEED
1 teaspoon green tea or 1 teabag • 1 teaspoon dried jasmine flowers • 3 cloves
juice of ½ lemon • 5cm pared strip of lemon peel • 1 teaspoon honey

This tea is good to serve after a meal as it aids digestion. Do not drink jasmine tea while pregnant.

So *Soothing* **AR** *Anxiety reducing* **I** *Immunising*

Pour a cup of boiling water over the green tea, dried jasmine and cloves and leave to steep for 3–5 minutes, stirring frequently. Strain into a cup, add the lemon juice, lemon peel and honey, stir well and sip slowly.

NETTLE TEA WITH ORANGE

Serves: 1 - Steeping time: 3 minutes

YOU NEED
1 teaspoon dried nettle leaves or 1 teabag • 5cm pared strip of orange peel
1 teaspoon honey • 1 slice of orange

Nettles can help relieve arthritic symptoms.

 Immunising  Skin enhancing  Kidney cleansing

Pour a cup of boiling water over nettle leaves and orange peel and leave for 3 minutes. Strain into a cup, add honey then stir. Add the orange slice and sip slowly.

OLIVE LEAF TEA WITH SAFFRON

Serves: 1 - Steeping time: 6 minutes

YOU NEED

1 teaspoon dried olive leaf tea or 1 teabag • pinch of saffron powder
1 teaspoon honey

Olive leaves help lower blood sugar levels, which can help with diabetes.

E *Energising* **I** *Immunising* **BC** *Boosts circulation*

Pour a cup of boiling water over the olive leaf tea and saffron and leave to steep for 6 minutes. Strain into a cup, add the honey and stir. Sip slowly.

ICED PEACH ROOIBOS TEA

Serves: 2 - Steeping time: 3 minutes

YOU NEED
1 teaspoon rooibos tea or 1 teabag • 250ml fresh peach juice
1 slice of peach • 1 slice of lemon • 2 fresh mint sprigs • ice cubes

This tea contains copper, which can help the body in the absorption of iron.

ME *Mineral enriching* **Ao** *Anti-oxidising* **BC** *Boosts circulation*

Pour a cup of boiling water over the rooibos tea and leave for 3 minutes. Strain into a cup and cool. Add the peach juice, lemon slice, peach slice and mint. Stir and add ice cubes. Serve immediately.

RASPBERRY LEAF ICED TEA

Serves: 1 - Steeping time: 5 minutes

YOU NEED

18 raspberries • 1 teaspoon dried raspberry leaves or 1 teabag
2 cloves • 1 cinnamon stick • 5cm pared slice of lemon peel • 2 cucumber slices
1 fresh mint sprig • 1 teaspoon honey (optional) • ice cubes

Raspberry leaves are well known to help prepare mothers for childbirth as it is an effective uterine stimulant. Do not drink this tea in the early stages of pregnancy.

(D) *Aids digestion* **(K)** *Kidney cleansing* **(T)** *Helps sore throats*

Pour a cup of boiling water over leaves, 6 raspberries, cinnamon and cloves. Add lemon peel and stir. Leave for 5 minutes. Strain into a cup and cool. Pour into blender with remaining raspberries, cucumber and mint. Blend, strain and add ice.

ICED GREEN TEA WITH STRAWBERRIES

Serves: 1 - Steeping time: 3 minutes + 8 minutes boiling

YOU NEED

1 teaspoon green tea or 1 teabag • 6 strawberries, hulled and quartered
5cm pared strip of lemon peel • 1 teaspoon honey • ice cubes

This tea is good for your heart and helps lower cholesterol.

 *Anti-oxidising* *Diuretic* *Healing*

Pour a cup of boiling water over the green tea and leave to steep for 3 minutes.
Strain, add the lemon peel and cool. Put the strawberries into a pan with
2 tablespoons water and the honey. Boil for 8 minutes until strawberries are soft.
Strain into a glass, pour over the cooled tea with lemon and top up with ice.

ICED BLACK TEA WITH ORANGE

Serves: 1 - Steeping time: 4 minutes

YOU NEED

1 teaspoon black tea or 1 teabag • 2 x 5cm pared strips of orange peel
1 cinnamon stick • juice of ½ orange • 1 teaspoon honey • ice cubes

Black tea contains antioxidants different from that of fruit and vegetables, therefore can provide additional benefits.

E *Energising* **SR** *Stress relieving* **D** *Aids digestion*

Pour a cup of boiling water over the black tea, orange peel and cinnamon. Leave to steep for 4 minutes then strain. Add the orange juice and honey, stir and cool completely. Once cooled, strain over ice.

ICED WHITE TEA WITH PEACHES

Serves: 1 - Steeping time: 4 minutes

YOU NEED

1 teaspoon white tea or 1 teabag • 1 peach, peeled, stoned and diced
2.5cm piece ginger, peeled and bruised • juice of ½ lemon • 1 teaspoon honey
1 fresh mint sprig • ice cubes

White tea has antibacterial properties that can protect the body from various infection-forming bacteria, whereas peaches are high in vitamins and fibre.

Cl *Cleansing* **Rh** *Rehydrating* **D** *Aids digestion*

Pour a cup of boiling water over the white tea. Leave to steep for 4 minutes then strain into a cup, stir and cool completely. Mix the lemon, ginger and honey together. Blend the honey mixture with the diced peach and put into a glass. Strain over the cooled tea, add mint and top up with ice.

RED CLOVER ICED TEA WITH YUZU

Serves: 1 - Steeping time: 5 minutes

YOU NEED

1 teaspoon red clover tea or 1 teabag • 2 fresh mint sprigs
juice and grated zest of ½ lemon • 1 teaspoon honey
2 drops of yuzu • ice cubes

If you suffer from psoriasis, eczema or sunburn, it is good to use cooled clover tea as a lotion. Yuzu is high in antioxidants and vitamin C.

A *Anti-inflammatory* **D** *Aids digestion* **I** *Immunising*

Pour a cup of boiling water over the clover tea. Leave to steep for 5 minutes then strain into a cup. Add the lemon zest and juice, mint, yuzu and honey and cool completely. Stir, strain into a glass and top up with ice.

FRESH LEAF TEAS

*Made from fresh herbs and wild flowers,
these homemade leaf teas bring you
vitality and longevity.*

Honeysuckle • Bay leaf, cinnamon & orange
Wild chicory & orange • Pomegranate peel &
cardamom • Sage & clove • Catmint with lemon
verbena • Celery & fennel • Rosemary
Clover, honey & lemon • Fennel & basil
Mint & lemon verbena • Lavender & ginger
Lemon verbena • Marjoram & basil • Parsley &
celery • Fresh olive leaf with cinnamon
Iced basil leaf tea with pineapple

HONEYSUCKLE

Serves: 1 - Steeping time: 5 minutes

YOU NEED
1 handful of honeysuckle flowers and leaves • 1 teaspoon honey

Honeysuckle can be helpful in treating coughs and mild symptoms of asthma.

Ab *Antibacterial* **De** *Detoxifying* **So** *Soothing*

Pour a cup of boiling water over all the ingredients and leave to steep for 5 minutes. Stir, strain into a cup and sip slowly.

BAY LEAF, CINNAMON & ORANGE

Serves: 1 - Steeping time: 5 minutes

YOU NEED
2 bay leaves • 2.5cm pared slice of orange peel
½ orange slice • pinch of ground cinnamon

Bay leaves can help relieve headaches.

A *Anti-inflammatory* **Rh** *Rehydrating* **D** *Aids digestion*

Pour a cup of boiling water over the bay leaves, cinnamon and orange peel. Leave to steep for 5 minutes. Strain into a cup, add the orange slice, stir and sip slowly.

WILD CHICORY & ORANGE

Serves: 1 - Steeping time: 5 minutes

YOU NEED

1 small handful of wild chicory leaves and flowers • 5cm piece of orange peel

½ teaspoon honey

Chicory contains vitamins B, C, K and flavonoids.

Bp *Blood purifying* **L** *Liver cleansing* **MR** *Metabolism regulating*

Pour a cup of boiling water over all the ingredients and leave to steep for 5 minutes.
Strain into a cup, stir and sip slowly.

POMEGRANATE PEEL & CARDAMOM

Serves: 1 - Steeping time: 5 minutes

YOU NEED
5cm pared slice of orange peel

½ small pomegranate, broken up into 4 or 5 pieces, including the seeds

1 cardamom pod, crushed • 1 teaspoon green tea or 1 teabag

Pomegranate peel contains a large amount of antioxidants, including a high level of vitamin C.

De *Detoxifying*　**V** *Vitamin enriching*　**SE** *Skin enhancing*

Pour a cup of boiling water over all the ingredients and leave to steep for 5 minutes. Strain into a cup, stir and sip slowly.

SAGE & CLOVE

Serves: 1 - Steeping time: 5 minutes

YOU NEED

10 cloves, lightly crushed • 4 fresh sage leaves
1 teaspoon honey • 1 slice of lemon

This tea is great during exams or any kind of test as it boosts your memory.

Rx *Relaxing* **D** *Aids digestion* **So** *Soothing*

Pour a cup of boiling water over the sage and cloves and leave to steep for 5 minutes. Strain into a cup, add lemon and honey and stir. Sip slowly.

CATMINT WITH LEMON VERBENA

Serves: 1 - Steeping time: 5 minutes

YOU NEED
5cm fresh catmint sprig • 5cm fresh lemon verbena sprig

2 green cardamom pods, crushed • pinch of ground cinnamon • 1 teaspoon hone

Catmint will soothe an upset stomach.

So *Soothing* **D** *Aids digestion* **V** *Vitamin enriching*

Add the catmint, lemon verbena and cardamom pods to a teapot and pour in 1 cup of boiling water. Leave to steep for 5 minutes. Strain into a cup, add the honey and stir. Sprinkle with the cinnamon and sip slowly.

CELERY & FENNEL

Serves: 1 - Steeping time: 5 minutes

YOU NEED
3 celery leaves • ¼ teaspoon fennel seeds • 1 teaspoon celery seeds
1 teaspoon honey • ½ lemon, squeezed

Celery is a good herb to flush out toxins from the body.

 Bone enhancing **De** Detoxifying **Cl** Cleansing

Pour a cup of boiling water over all the ingredients and leave to stand for 5 minutes. Strain into a cup, stir and sip slowly.

ROSEMARY

Serves: 1 - Steeping time: 5 minutes

YOU NEED

5cm fresh rosemary sprig • 5cm pared strip of orange peel
4 cloves • 1 teaspoon honey • 1 teaspoon lemon juice

Rosemary is a great herb for helping with depression and anxiety.

E *Energising*   **A** *Anti-inflammatory*   **R** *Rejuvenating*

Pour a cup of boiling water over all the ingredients and leave to steep for 5 minutes.
Strain into a cup, stir and sip slowly.

CLOVER, HONEY & LEMON

Serves: 1 - Steeping time: 5 minutes

YOU NEED

5 fresh red clover flowers • 1 teaspoon honey

juice of ½ lemon

It is called red clover even though the flowers are pink. This herb is known to help boost fertility. Drink this tea on a regular basis over a few years.

Cl *Cleansing* **So** *Soothing* **R** *Rejuvenating*

Pour a cup of boiling water over all the ingredients and leave for 5 minutes. Strain into a cup, stir and sip slowly.

FENNEL & BASIL

Serves: 1 - Steeping time: 5 minutes

YOU NEED

1 tablespoon fresh fennel fronds • 1 teaspoon fennel seeds

4 fresh basil leaves • 1 teaspoon apple cider vinegar

Fennel helps relieve fluid retention and is a great all-round cleanser.

De *Detoxifying* **D** *Aids digestion* **Di** *Diuretic*

Pour a cup of boiling water over all the ingredients and leave to steep for
5 minutes. Strain into a cup, stir and sip slowly.

MINT & LEMON VERBENA

Serves: 1 - Steeping time: 5 minutes

YOU NEED

1 tablespoon fresh mint leaves • 1 tablespoon fresh lemon verbena leaves

Mint is a well-known to help ease indigestion.

De *Detoxifying* **L** *Liver cleansing* **St** *Stimulating*

Put leaves into a teapot and pour in a cup of boiling water. Leave to steep for
5 minutes. Strain into a cup, stir and sip slowly.

LAVENDER & GINGER

Serves: 1 - Steeping time: 5 minutes

YOU NEED
2.5cm piece of ginger, peeled and sliced • 2 fresh lavender sprigs
3 cardamom pods, lightly crushed • 1 teaspoon honey

Lavender can help you sleep and ease anxiety.

Rx *Relaxing* **R** *Rejuvenating* **Me** *Mood enhancing*

Put the lavender, ginger and cardamom pods in a teapot and pour in a cup of
boiling water. Leave for 5 minutes. Strain into a cup, add honey, stir and sip slowly.

LEMON VERBENA

Serves: 1 - Steeping time: 4 minutes

YOU NEED

2.5cm piece of ginger, peeled and sliced • 60g fresh lemon verbena leaves
5cm pared slice of lemon peel • 1 teaspoon honey

Lemon verbena is an excellent herb for treating stress.

 **D** *Aids digestion* **Me** *Mood enhancing* **So** *Soothing*

Put the lemon verbena, ginger and lemon peel into a teapot and pour in a cup of boiling water. Leave to steep for 4 minutes then strain into a cup. Add the honey and stir. Sip slowly. It is also delicious cold, just add ice cubes.

MARJORAM & BASIL

Serves: 1 - Steeping time: 5 minutes

YOU NEED
2 fresh basil leaves • 1 tablespoon fresh marjoram leaves
1 teaspoon honey • 1 teaspoon lemon juice

Majoram is a wonderful herb that can help lift your spirits and soothe your aches and pains.

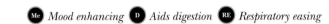 *Mood enhancing*  *Aids digestion*  *Respiratory easing*

Pour a cup of boiling water over the marjoram and basil. Add the lemon juice and honey, stir and leave to steep for 5 minutes. Strain into a cup, stir and sip slowly.

PARSLEY & CELERY

Serves: 1 - Steeping time: 5 minutes

YOU NEED

60g fresh flat-leaf parsley • 60g fresh celery leaves

5cm fresh thyme sprig • 1 teaspoon lightly crushed coriander seeds

1 slice of lemon

This is a great diuretic and good for the morning after a big night.

V *Vitamin enriching* **K** *Kidney cleansing* **De** *Detoxifying*

Pour a cup of boiling water over all the ingredients and leave to steep for 5 minutes.
Strain into a cup, stir and sip slowly.

FRESH OLIVE LEAF WITH CINNAMON

Serves: 1 - Steeping time: 5 minutes

YOU NEED
60g fresh olive sprigs • 2 teaspoons apple cider vinegar • 1 cinnamon stick

Olive leaves can help boost immunity.

CB *Circulation boosting* **BR** *Blood regulating* **E** *Energising*

Put the olive sprigs in a teapot and pour in a cup of boiling water. Leave to steep for 5 minutes. Strain into a cup and add the vinegar. Stir with the cinnamon stick for added subtle flavour. Sip slowly.

ICED BASIL LEAF TEA WITH PINEAPPLE

Serves: 1 - Steeping time: 3 minutes

YOU NEED

60g fresh basil leaves • 2cm thick slice of peeled pineapple
6 thin slices of unpeeled cucumber • ice cubes

Basil tea is great to drink after a meal for its detoxifying properties.

CI *Cleansing*   **BE** *Blood enhancing*   **A** *Anti-inflammatory*

Pour a cup of boiling water over the basil leaves and leave to steep for 3 minutes. Strain and cool. In a blender, blend the cucumber and pineapple with the ice. Pour into a glass, pour the basil tea over the top and serve.

GREEN TONICS

These tonics are invigorating, refreshing and restorative. They are full of health benefits to ease a variety of ailments and are made with fresh ingredients, strong in flavour and should be sipped slowly.

Clover, lemon & sage • Green tea tonic with lemon peel • Simple lemon • Marjoram & ginger Mint, caraway & fennel • Nutmeg & ginger Oregano & ginger • Rosehip & cinnamon Rosemary & honey • Sage & peppermint Stevia & elderberries • Turmeric • Saffron, honey & coconut • Spirulina & peppermint • Cacao & cayenne • Valerian root & lavender Spiced almond & date • Maca & pecan

CLOVER, LEMON & SAGE

Serves: 1 - Simmering time: 8 minutes

YOU NEED

60g fresh sage leaves • 3 tablespoons fresh clover flowers or 1½ tablespoons clover tea
pared rind and juice of ½ lemon • 2 teaspoons honey • 10 cloves

This tonic can help soothe a cough.

So *Soothing* **E** *Energising* **D** *Aids digestion*

n a saucepan, add the clover, lemon rind, sage and cloves. Add 2 cups of water and
ring to the boil. Simmer for 8 minutes. Strain and add the lemon juice and honey.
Drink ½ cup warm tonic 4 times a day.

GREEN TEA TONIC WITH LEMON PEEL

Serves: 1 - Steeping time: 6–7 minutes

YOU NEED
2 tablespoons green tea or 1 teabag • 5cm pared strip of lemon peel
1 teaspoon honey • 1 tablespoon lemon juice

Green tea is full of antioxidants that help boost the immune system.

I *Immunising* **Di** *Diuretic* **K** *Kidney cleansing*

Pour a cup of boiling water over all the ingredients and leave to steep for 6–7 minutes. Strain, stir and sip. If you are using tea leaves, don't discard them, as they can be used for the next couple of cups.

SIMPLE LEMON

Serves: 1 - Steeping time: 3 minutes

YOU NEED

6 slices of lemon • pared rind of 1 lemon • 2 teaspoons honey

Lemon is a very good blood cleanser and has antibacterial properties.

V *Vitamin enriching* **A** *Anti-inflammatory* **Al** *Alkalising*

Pour 2 cups of boiling water over lemon rind and slices and leave to steep for
minutes. Stir well, strain and add the honey. Sip ½ cup tonic every 3 hours. Can be
enjoyed warm or cold.

MARJORAM & GINGER

Serves: 1 - Steeping time: 5 minutes

YOU NEED

2 tablespoons fresh marjoram leaves • 2.5cm piece of ginger, peeled and chopped

2 tablespoons fresh lemon verbena leaves • ½ lemon, squeezed • 4 cloves

4 fresh mint leaves • 2 teaspoons honey

This tonic soothes heartburn, aching muscles and helps you sleep.

D *Aids digestion*   **A** *Antibacterial*   **So** *Soothing*

Pour 2 cups of boiling water over the marjoram, lemon verbena, ginger and cloves.
Now add the lemon, mint and honey and stir. Leave to steep for 5 minutes.
Sip ½ cup hot tonic 4 times a day.

MINT, CARAWAY & FENNEL

Serves: 1 - Steeping time: 5 minutes

YOU NEED
2 tablespoons fresh mint leaves • 2 tablespoons fresh lemon verbena leaves
1 teaspoon caraway seeds, lightly crushed • 1 teaspoon fennel seeds, lightly crushed

This tonic is great for any type of indigestion.

 Cleansing  Detoxifying  Soothing

Put all the ingredients into a teapot and pour over 2 cups of boiling water.
Leave to steep for 5 minutes. Strain. Sip ¼ cup warm tonic 3–4 times a day.

NUTMEG & GINGER

Serves: 1 - Steeping time: 5 minutes

YOU NEED

1 teaspoon freshly grated nutmeg • 2 tablespoons freshly grated ginger

½ lemon, squeezed

This tonic will help soothe aches and pains. Note that nutmeg is potent, so do not drink this tea every day.

 *Aids digestion*  *Skin repairing*  *Soothing*

Pour 2 cups of boiling water over the nutmeg and ginger and stir through the lemon juice. Leave to steep for 5 minutes. Strain. Sip ½ cup hot tonic 3–4 times a day.

OREGANO & GINGER

Serves: 1 - Steeping time: 8 minutes

YOU NEED
2 tablespoons fresh oregano leaves • 1 garlic clove, sliced
2.5cm piece of ginger, peeled and grated • ½ lemon, squeezed

This tonic is as good as an antibiotic.

IF *Infection fighting* **V** *Vitamin enriching* **Rf** *Refreshing*

Pour 2 cups of boiling water over all the ingredients and leave to steep for
8 minutes. Strain. Sip ½ cup warm or cold tonic 4 times a day.

ROSEHIP & CINNAMON

Serves: 1 - Steeping time: 5 minutes

YOU NEED

4 tablespoons dried rosehips • 2.5cm pared strip of lemon peel

juice of ½ lemon • 1 teaspoon grated ginger

½ teaspoon ground cinnamon • 1 teaspoon honey

Rosehip has a fragrant taste and can ease tension and fatigue.

I *Immunising* **D** *Aids digestion* **SR** *Stress reducing*

Put the rosehips, lemon peel and ginger into a teapot. Pour over 2 cups of boiling
water and add the lemon juice and honey and stir. Leave to steep for 5 minutes.
Strain. Drink ½ cup warm or cold tonic 4 times a day.

ROSEMARY & HONEY

Serves: 1 - Steeping time: 7 minutes

YOU NEED

1 fresh rosemary sprig • 1 teaspoon honey

A pure tonic of rosemary helps you to restore a positive outlook.

R *Rejuvenating* **A** *Anti-inflammatory* **BS** *Blood stimulating*

Pour 2 cups of boiling water over the rosemary and leave to steep for 7 minutes.
Add the honey and stir. Strain. Drink ½ cup warm or cold tonic 4 times a day.

SAGE & PEPPERMINT

Serves: 1 - Steeping time: 6 minutes

YOU NEED
5cm fresh peppermint sprig • 12 fresh sage leaves
½ lemon, squeezed • 1 teaspoon honey

This is a tonic to help enhance memory as well as being comforting. Do not drink for longer than 10 days without a 2–3 day break.

So *Soothing* **D** *Aids digestion* **Rf** *Refreshing*

Pour 2 cups of boiling water over the sage and peppermint and leave to steep for 6 minutes. Add the honey and lemon and stir. Sip ½ cup hot tonic 4 times a day.

STEVIA & ELDERBERRIES

Serves: 1 - Simmering time: 15 minutes

YOU NEED

2 tablespoons stevia sprigs, chopped • 2 tablespoons dried elderberries

5cm pared strip of lemon peel

This tonic can help with fatigue.

E *Energising* **BR** *Blood regulating* **Ab** *Antibacterial*

Put all the ingredients into a pan with 440ml water and slowly bring to the boil.
Cover and simmer for 15 minutes. Strain. Sip ½ cup warm or cold tonic twice a day.

TURMERIC

Serves: 1 - Simmering time: 15 minutes

YOU NEED

2 teaspoons ground turmeric • 1 teaspoon anise

½ lemon juice • 440ml coconut water

This tonic is a great digestive and helps cleanse the liver.

D *Aids digestion* **A** *Anti-inflammatory* **CR** *Cholesterol reducing*

Put all the ingredients into a pan and slowly bring to a simmer. Simmer for 15 minutes. Strain. Sip ½ cup warm or cold tonic 4 times a day.

SAFFRON, HONEY & COCONUT

Serves: 1 - Simmering time: 15 minutes

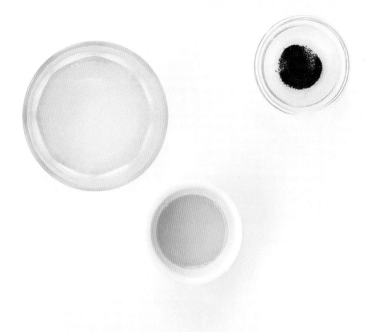

YOU NEED

pinch of saffron strands • 440ml coconut water • 1 teaspoon honey

Saffron is a good antidepressant herb.

BR *Blood regulating* **D** *Aids digestion* **C** *Calming*

Put all the ingredients into a pan and slowly bring to a simmer for 15 minutes. Turn off, stir and strain. Sip ½ cup warm or cold tonic 4 times a day.

SPIRULINA & PEPPERMINT

Serves: 1 - Steeping time: 5 minutes

YOU NEED

2 tablespoons fresh peppermint leaves

2 tablespoons spirulina • ½ lemon, squeezed

Spirulina is rich in antioxidants and helps strengthen the immune system.

Cl *Cleansing* **Bb** *Blood building* **A** *Anti-inflammatory*

Pour 2 cups of boiling water over the ingredients and leave to steep for 5 minutes.
Strain. Sip ½ cup hot or cold tonic 4 times a day.

CACAO & CAYENNE

Serves: 1 - Steeping time: 5 minutes

YOU NEED

1 tablespoon cacao nibs • 1 teaspoon honey • pinch of cayenne pepper

Cayenne pepper helps you kickstart your body into action, making it a good tonic to fire you up.

E *Energising* **SB** *Stamina boosting* **Bb** *Blood boosting*

Pour 2 cups of boiling water over the cacao and cayenne and leave to steep for 5 minutes. Stir in honey and strain. Sip ½ cup warm or cold tonic every 4 hours.

VALERIAN ROOT & LAVENDER

Serves: 1 - Steeping time: 8 minutes

YOU NEED
1 tablespoon lavender • 1 tablespoon valerian root • 1 tablespoon honey

This sleepy tonic makes sure you get a good night in bed.

AR *Anxiety reducing* **C** *Calming* **So** *Soothing*

Pour 2 cups of boiling water over all the ingredients and leave to steep for 8 minutes. Strain and stir. Sip ½ cup warm or cold tonic 4 times a day.

SPICED ALMOND & DATE

Serves: 1 - Cooking time: 15 minutes

YOU NEED

2 tablespoons almonds • 3 dates, stoned • 1 teaspoon ground cinnamon

Almonds are thought to increase your libido while dates can boost your energy.

E *Energising* **SB** *Stamina boosting* **C** *Calming*

Put all the ingredients into a blender with 1 cup of water and blend until smooth.
Put this into a pan along with another cup of water and slowly bring to the boil for
15 minutes. Strain. Drink ½ cup warm tonic every 4 hours.

MACA & PECAN

Serves: 1 - Cooking time: 15 minutes

YOU NEED
2 tablespoons maca root powder • 1 tablespoon pecan nuts
1 teaspoon honey

Maca root is good at balancing hormones and increasing endurance.

R *Rejuvenating* **Cl** *Cleansing* **Bb** *Blood building*

In a blender, blend the pecans and maca root powder with 1 cup of cold water until smooth. Put this into a pan along with the honey. Slowly bring to the boil for 15 minutes. Take off the heat and strain. Drink ½ cup warm tonic every 4 hours.

CLEANSERS

These drinks are full of refreshing and light ingredients to help the body detoxify and rehydrate.

Chia, cucumber & aloe vera • Lemon thyme &
melon cleanser • Parsley & watermelon
Celery cleanser • Cucumber & mint
Burdock root & coriander

CHIA, CUCUMBER & ALOE VERA

Serves: 1 - Chilling time: 8 hours

YOU NEED
½ cucumber, sliced • 2 tablespoons aloe vera

1 tablespoon chia seeds

This cleanser is full of omega-3 fatty acids and a little bit of protein.

De *Detoxifying* **R** *Rehydrating* **Cl** *Cleansing*

Put the ingredients into a jug or Kilner jar with 300ml water and chill overnight.
Shake or stir in the morning and sip throughout the day.

LEMON THYME & MELON CLEANSER

Serves: 1 - Cooling time: 30 minutes

YOU NEED

100g green melon, such as honeydew, cut into bite-sized pieces
20g fresh lemon thyme sprigs • 240ml white grape juice • ice cubes

This rejuvenating cleanser eases backache and stiff shoulders.

So *Soothing*　**BS** *Blood stimulating*　**I** *Immunising*

Blend the melon with the grape juice in a blender. Pour a cup of boiling water over the lemon thyme then leave to cool and strain into a cup. Combine with the melon and grape juice and sip over ice.

PARSLEY & WATERMELON

Serves: 1 - Preparation time: 5 minutes

YOU NEED

15g parsley, stalks included • juice of 1 lemon

1 cucumber, peeled and chopped • 250g watermelon

Parsley contains high amounts of vitamin C and calcium.

Rf *Refreshing* **H** *Hydrating* **V** *Vitamin enhancing*

Blend all the ingredients together in a blender and top up with water if needed. Strain into a cup and serve.

CELERY CLEANSER

Serves: 1 - Steeping time: 5 minutes

YOU NEED

30g celery leaves • 15g fennel leaves • 1 teaspoon celery seeds
2 carrots, roughly chopped • 5 fresh parsley sprigs • 10 slices of cucumber
juice of 1 lemon

This cleanser is high in calcium.

Cl *Cleansing* **De** *Detoxifying* **R** *Rejuvenating*

Put the carrots, cucumber and parsley into a blender with 50ml water and blend. Strain into a jug. Pour a cup of boiling water over the celery and fennel leaves, add the celery seeds and leave to steep for 5 minutes, then strain and cool. Add the carrot juice mixture and stir well. Add the lemon juice and serve chilled.

CUCUMBER & MINT

Serves: 1 - Steeping time: 1 hour

YOU NEED

½ cucumber, sliced • 1 teaspoon grated ginger

pinch of cayenne pepper • 1 handful of mint leaves

juice of 1 lime • ice cubes

This cleanser is high in vitamins A, C and K, as well as calcium and potassium.

 Rehydrating  Anti-inflammatory  Aids digestion

Put all the ingredients into a jug and pour over cold water. Leave to steep for
1 hour. Serve over ice.

BURDOCK ROOT & CORIANDER

Serves: 1 - Steeping time: 5 minutes

YOU NEED

1 tablespoon burdock root • ½ cucumber, sliced

2 celery sticks, halved and chopped

1 teaspoon ground coriander • ½ lemon, sliced

Burdock root can be used to help with high blood pressure and joint pain.

P *Purifying* **SE** *Skin enhancing* **A** *Anti-inflammatory*

Pour 2 cups boiling water over the burdock root and leave to steep for 5 minutes. Strain and cool. Blend the tea with the celery sticks, coriander and cucumber in a blender until smooth. Pour into a glass, add lemon slices to taste, stir well and sip.

INDEX

IMPORTANT NOTE TO READERS: Although every effort has been made to ensure that the contents of this book are accurate, it must not be treated as a substitute for qualified medical advice. Always consult a qualified medical practitioner. Neither the authors nor the publisher can be held responsible for any loss or claim arising out of the use, or misuse, of the suggestions made or the failure to take professional medical advice.

hachette
AUSTRALIA

Published in Australia and New Zealand in 2016
by Hachette Australia
(an imprint of Hachette Australia Pty Limited)
Level 17, 207 Kent Street, Sydney NSW 2000
www.hachette.com.au

10 9 8 7 6 5 4 3 2 1

Cataloguing-in-Publication data is available from the National Library of Australia.

978 0 7336 3605 9(pbk.)

Acknowledgements

Firstly, I'd like to thank Mirabilia for their lovely dried olive leaf tea from Abruzzo, Italy (www.oleaft.com); Tom Westerich for the use of his fantastic studio, Deirdre Rooney for great photos and a fantastic shoot; Kathy Steer for her patience and Michelle Tilly for the design. This has been a fun book to create, thank you Catie Ziller for making it happen.

The author has researched each plant used in this book but is not responsible for any adverse effects any of the plants may have on an individual. One plant may be good for one person but have a negative effect on another. All the plants are consumed entirely at your own risk. Never use a plant as an alternative to seeking professional medical advice and always consume tea in moderation.

Publisher: Catie Ziller   Author: Fern Green
Designer: Michelle Tilly   Photographer: Deirdre Rooney
Editor: Kathy Steer

Colour reproduction by Splitting Image
Printed in China by Toppan Leefung Printing Limited